# HOW TO GET
# ARRESTED

*A Motivational Story for*
## ACTORS

## By Michael J. Wallach

authorHOUSE™

1663 LIBERTY DRIVE, SUITE 200
BLOOMINGTON, INDIANA 47403
(800) 839-8640
WWW.AUTHORHOUSE.COM

"How To Get Arrested" and "Arrested Publications" are trademarks of Michael J. Wallach.

No part of this book may be reproduced, stored in a retrieval system, or transmitted by any means without the written permission of the author.

First published by AuthorHouse 09/08/05

ISBN: 1-4208-8014-4 (e)
ISBN: 1-4208-7903-0 (sc)
ISBN: 1-4208-7902-2 (dj)

Library of Congress Control Number: 2005907653

Printed in the United States of America
Bloomington, Indiana

This book is printed on acid-free paper.

*To my loving brother Tom*

*To the thousands of actors striving for success*

**ILLUSTRATIONS AND COVER DESIGN BY**
*Paul Thurwachter*

**DESIGN ENHANCEMENT**
*Joshua H. Schuyler*

**COVER PHOTO**
*Mario R. Prado*


**SPECIAL THANKS:**

*Tom Wallach*
*Brittany Wallach*
*Jacqueline Wallach*
*Maggie Wallach*
*Carolyn Howard-Johnson*
*Alan L. Gansberg*
*Joanne Baron*
*Helene Sokol*
*Judy Kerr*
*Dan Pahlajani*
*Les Abell*
*Carolyn Cable*
*Allen Fawcett*
*Madaline Blau*
*Barbara Grossman*
*Michael Hamilburg*
*John Bradshaw*

# CHAPTERS

# Flying To LA

Dick and Jane sit arm-by-arm on a jet plane high above the clouds. Thirty-three thousand feet to be exact. Not only are their bodies high up in the sky, but so are their minds. Each is dreaming about a career in a far off land. Los Angeles is about to become the home of these two actors.

Pursuing acting in New York had been exciting. There were lots of ways for Dick and Jane to stay busy by attending classes, going to plays, or "knocking on doors." In Manhattan, they would sometimes take their pictures and resumes, walk right into a manager's, agent's or casting director's office and present themselves. "Hi, I'm Dick and I came up here to drop off my picture. Please check it out." That felt good. Dick did something for himself. Now, he can look at his list of offices and find the next one to go to. "Oh yeah, the one on 43rd Street is close by so I'll go up there."

So, in N.Y., Dick and Jane and other actors looking for work have tons of possibilities to stay active and pursue their business. Plenty of offices, and they are all within walking distance or easy enough to get to by taking a subway, bus or cab. Dick could plan a whole day of dropping off pictures. And, by doing so, there was always the hope that someone would see him and call him into the office right then and there! "Hey, don't leave, Dick, come in here and read for this part," a casting director might say. Or, after his picture and resume is perused, Dick might get a call to come back to read for a part in a project that they are casting.

In New York you could feel that something has been accomplished, as opposed to sitting around your apartment all day waiting for the phone to ring while pulling out your hair. You walk along the streets running into other actors who you can converse with.

You can discuss jobs that are out there, gossip and learn. You may stroll past Broadway theatres, movie marquees, work out in a gym, or hang out in Starbucks, Barnes & Noble or Borders alongside others pursuing acting. Maybe you spot a well-known actor who's working in town.

It's great to get out there. Feel you might be achieving something. Feel you are part of the "community." But in L.A., offices are miles and miles apart. You need a car and enough time to navigate through the heavy traffic. So, it's harder to feel that you are getting something done. Distance and isolation make that sense of community tough to achieve. In L.A., the true feeling of accomplishment is more easily felt when you are actually getting acting jobs. As for the ways of becoming a working actor, answers will unfold throughout this story. (Be aware that the same basic principles that you will read apply to succeeding anywhere and in any business.)

Back to our heroes. Dick and Jane's excitement builds knowing they're an hour away from N.Y and that much closer to Hollywood. Dick daydreams of being discovered when he strolls through the airport terminal. In fact, he thinks that before he even arrives, walking down the aisle to the men's lavatory could get him discovered by a producer flying to L.A. Jane, on the other hand, looks over a list of Los Angeles agents. She hopes that she gets represented by one who keeps her working regularly.

Time for lunch. A big smile comes over Dick's face as he checks out the tray of food just handed him by the flight attendant. He notices a piece of cake under the plastic wrap and gobbles it up before starting on the salad. He pours the cup of salad dressing over the lettuce and asks for another before beginning. Next, he slathers two pats of butter on the tiny bun and salts the chicken slices. He pops the can of a sugary Coke and downs it.

When Jane made the ticket reservation, she requested a special meal. A plate of fruit is on her tray. Jane finishes her fruit and dabs her forefinger into the cake and licks it off, and washes down the meal with her bottled water. Still thirsty, Dick takes out a few dollars for beer and reaches for the candy bars he purchased in the terminal. As Dick lets out a burp, Jane winces.

Dick and Jane are friends from New York. They met in an acting class in the Village and bonded. They talked often after classes and hung out together whenever they could. They confided in each other. Jane told Dick about her past relationships. Dick told Jane about his many misfires. While a close companionship resulted, romance never entered into it. They wanted to concentrate on their careers, especially Jane.

In discussing their careers, they decided that they had done about all they could do as actors there. Both had done off-off-Broadway plays. Jane did a couple of days on soap operas and Dick did a recurring role on a soap. They each did a couple of commercials. Both modeled a bit too. There are some TV shows in N.Y. like "Law & Order," but neither landed guest starring work on a series. As for feature films, relatively few are made or cast in N.Y., so they didn't fare well in that medium either. They figured that their chances were better on the West Coast where scores of series and features are cast and filmed.

Calculations were made regarding living expenses necessary to live in Los Angeles. While apartment rents would be less than in New York, it would be necessary to buy a car. They wanted to save enough money so that they could pursue acting without having to "wait" tables for at least a few months. They worked slavishly taking on additional shifts. Sufficient funds were accumulated. They would share one car. They were ready, at least financially.

Both Dick and Jane are good-looking enough to work in the very competitive world of acting although casting is not limited to good looks. Anybody can work in the business. There are roles for all types. Where there is a Brad Pitt there is also a Danny DeVito. Where there is a Heather Locklear there is also a Kathy Bates. More: a George Clooney and a James Gandolfini, a Halle Berry and a Whoopi Goldberg, Rob Lowe and Ben Stiller, Lucy Liu and Queen Latifah, Jennifer Lopez and Roseanne Barr. The beat goes on.

Jane decides to stretch and takes a walk down the aisle. She is excited to be making this journey to L.A. She is also worried about not making it. She

has been preparing for this move for months. In New York, exclusivity is not always required by an agency and an actor usually works with several of them. Any of them can "send you out" on auditions. Jane has spoken with all of the agents she works with about her move. Some didn't want to lose her because they had spent time on her career and were making some money from their ten percent commission structure. They looked forward to capitalizing on her success when she eventually booked bigger jobs. Their thinking was that as time went on a TV pilot might be cast in town. Perhaps Jane would be right for it. They would get her an audition and Jane would be cast in it. That would mean lots of money, pride and prestige for the agent, particularly if the pilot went to series and the production company's option on Jane's acting services was "picked up." Everyone would be happy and rewarded.

Some of the people and agents that Jane spoke with felt that the LA lifestyle was so different. They also felt that Jane wasn't ready, that she should have more acting credits and training. More theatre especially on Broadway would be helpful. Some guest starring credits on episodes of TV shows or a meaty part in an "A" feature film would be good. But, while those credits would have been nice to have, others advised Jane to make her coastal move now. They thought Jane's age was a major consideration.

When possible, it is better to pursue acting at a young age simply because there are more roles available to actors who can play teenagers and young adults. Think of all the TV series and "coming of age" type feature films. A large majority of the roles are for young people. So, as long as Jane has adequate acting training and some credits many people "in the know" might advise her to make a move sooner rather than later. Of course, it would be more opportune if Jane had an important part in a studio or quality independent film coming out because the "industry" looks favorably on a new actor who has a strong chance of achieving immediate status and recognizability. But Jane was wise. She weighed her chances: If she waited for that pilot or movie and it didn't happen within a year or two, she would be relegated to coming out to L.A. at a disadvantage. She might not be able to play roles that require teenage and young adult looks. Occasionally an actress old enough to have a teenager is able to play a teenager herself, but that is rare. The same goes for the younger looking guy.

The "age thing" does not preclude an actor who starts his or her career at the age of 40, 50, 60, or 70, or is still struggling at those ages from making it. After forty years as a stuntman, Richard Farnsworth decided to pursue acting and at 58 won an Academy Award nomination for his role in "Comes A Horseman." He was nominated again in "The Straight Story" at 79. Estelle Getty did theatre and was unknown to the public until she was well into her sixties and landed a series role on "Golden Girls." If you are a mature actor but haven't yet achieved success, you never know when a big break may come. So you persist, keep believing, keep going, for the answer to your goal may be a phone call away.

Furthermore, although Jane was not fully aware of the reasons that L.A. presented more casting opportunities, her instincts were dead on. She noticed that her New York agents never got her auditions for roles in episodes of series shot in L.A. She felt that she was missing out. As for TV pilots, most of them are shot on the West Coast, in L.A. or Vancouver. While Jane knew of actors who were seen in N.Y. and subsequently flown out to L.A. by the studio or network producing the pilot, that happened infrequently, and she was never one of them. The fact is, whether it is a movie or TV production, most of the casting is done with actors based only a few miles away. The producer wants to make directors use a "local hire" whenever possible; it is a matter of expediency, money and convenience.

Enough with L.A. versus N.Y. Let's land this plane, get to our apartment, and learn about how to effectively pursue this business of acting.

# In The Cab
# To The Apartment

As the jet descends towards LAX, Dick and Jane gather up their carry-on bags, laptops, iPod and CD players. They proceed to baggage claim, grab their luggage off the conveyor belt, and head towards the exit doors. Jane looks for the cab line. Dick puts on his dark sunglasses. Off to West Hollywood where they were fortunate to have already sublet an inexpensive two bedroom apartment. Jane wants to live close to most of the studios, TV networks, casting directors, agents, managers and theatres where plays are performed by newer actors. Dick knew that was the right thing to do although he really wants to live at the beach near some of his actor buddies from N.Y.

The cab driver is also an actor. He explains to Dick and Jane that although the studios are all over L.A. -- from south of the airport in Manhattan Beach to way north in what people call "The Valley" and easterly to Burbank -- he thinks West Hollywood is a good place to live because it is centrally located. Living close to the action saves time. There is no point in blowing a hard-to-get appointment with tardiness. Coming late will not endear you to an agent nor does playing hard to get win you any points when you're trying to get a job.

The driver, who looks around 40 to Dick and Jane, tells them some of the mistakes that he made while pursuing an acting career and that he still seems to be making them. Neither of our heroes wants to be set back by making mistakes. They have no time to waste and more importantly, they don't want to miss any opportunities. As they reach the apartment complex the driver relates how an agent wined and dined him and told him how the agency would make him a star. He signed with the agent, but the audition appointments seemed to disappear after the first week. He is in the middle of telling them how he should have never left the previous agent who was getting him auditions and jobs when Dick jumps out of the cab because he doesn't like hearing this downer of a story. Jane wants to stay and listen because she is learning some real truth about the acting business, but Dick urges her to get out of the car and check out the apartment. She does so and wishes the cab driver luck in his acting career.

The apartment is just South of Sunset Boulevard. Jane picks out a bedroom and starts to set up her new life. She organizes her clothes, makeup, pictures and resumes, sets out her acting books and places her laptop computer on the desk. She is ready to get to business.

Dick sits in front of the TV and watches a soap opera. He recognizes an acquaintance who has landed a regular role on the show. "I can't believe that. How did he get that and not me? I'm better looking and have more talent than him. Hope he gets fired."

Dick's little outbreak is not good. Negativity and

desire for another to not do well, particularly if it's someone you know, is bad for your career, psyche, and impacts on your ability to fully enjoy your day. In fact, there's actually a word for Dick's actions. It's called "shaudenfreud." That's when you take pleasure in the discomfort of others especially friends and allies. What a waste of time and energy to be jealous and think ill towards another. And if you believe in karma, watch out. As for Dick, I wouldn't be surprised if it gnawed at him all day. Stay positive, it is an attribute that helps one succeed in any business.

With their phones and fax installed, their cell phones in hand and their laptops set up, Dick and Jane are ready to do combat.

# I Want To
# Be Someone's Client

What to do next? Jane starts her research. Gotta join an acting class. Gotta find an agent and maybe a manager too. Got to get in with this "community," but Jane can't just walk out of her house and run into people. Seems as though everybody and everything is so far apart. She buys actor-oriented newspapers such as *Back Stage West* and calls the Screen Actors Guild (SAG) for their advice. She speaks to virtually everyone she knows including New York friends and acquaintances and her acting teacher (whom she greatly misses). She looks at actor source books such as *Acting Is Everything* and researches the

Internet where she finds countless websites that have information concerning actors. One of them is www. actorsaccess.com where she can learn about actor-related events and actually "submit" herself for some of the roles being cast to which agents and managers are privy. She finds agents at www.agentassociation. com which is The Association of Talent Agents (ATA). She discovers an organization comprising some of the hundreds of managers called the Talent Managers Association (TMA) at www.talentmanagers.org.

Now, to utilize this information. Jane compiles a list of potential agents and managers. About half way through, she gets distracted when she hears a screeching tire noise coming out of the living room. Dick is playing a popular auto theft video game. Considering the way Dick has begun pursuing his career, it seems that, while he may be able to virtually steal some cars, it's unlikely he'll be able to snag an agent.

After putting together her lists, Jane starts to mail and email her picture and resume. Her photo (8 x 10 glossy) looks like her as opposed to one touched up to the point where there is no close resemblance. Remember that if you are called in to see a casting director under the pretense of an unrealistic picture, you cannot expect to be accorded proper consideration. A casting person, agent or manager who sees a picture and asks someone to come in for an audition or interview expects to see what was in the picture. If they wanted a different look they wouldn't have called you in. They do not want to be deceived. Not only will you waste their time and yours, but also you risk upsetting the interviewer and ruin your chances of representation or a callback for the role. It's no different with a potential employee for, say, a secretarial position. It is a risk to include false information about past employment on a resume or doctor letters of recommendation. Although an audition may not lead to being cast for the role, a good meeting (or reading) might keep you high in the casting director's mind. As a result, you could be called in for a future role or get your name bantered about to other casting directors as someone worth seeing. It's called a "buzz." And it's always nice when a casting person tells your representative about what a pleasure it was to meet you. (There will be more on the casting process later.)

Jane uploads her picture and resume into her computer. Doing so enables her to email her stuff to prospective agents, managers, and casting directors and to do so easily and inexpensively. For example, the website www.talentmanagers.org enables actors to email their pictures and resumes to its more than one hundred members. She can put her picture and resume online at www.actorsaccess.com making it possible for casting directors, agents and managers to view her materials with a simple mouse click. Jane can set up her own website. She can even put her "composite tape" online allowing others to view scenes from some of the shows in which she performed.

Dick takes a break from his TV schedule and wonders what Jane is up to. "May I look over your list?" he asks peering over her shoulder. Jane says sure and that she hopes it helps him.

Dick finds some names, puts together some packages and writes a cover letter to go with his picture and resume. It's a full-page single-spaced letter describing him and what he had done in New York along with his goals and aspirations and what he feels about the business. Was his long full-page cover letter helpful? No, not at all. When his package is opened, the recipient won't want to read an autobiography. These days nobody has time to read lengthy cover letters. Rather, it's about writing succinctly and to the point. The reader will want to know of the sender's request, the sender's important characteristic(s), the name of the person referring you if there is one, and professional credit(s), if you have any. Then, after reading the brief cover letter the reader will turn the page and look at the picture and resume. Representatives receive hundreds if not thousands of submissions so keep it simple if you want to increase your chances of having an interview set up.

Here are the results of Dick and Jane's submissions: Jane gets called in to meet with a few agents and managers; Dick never even receives a response.

It is a big day for Jane. She has an appointment with a small, credible and established L.A. agency, which we will call New Talent. She feels that she would look good in snug jeans and a t-shirt with some midriff showing but decides against it. Show some respect, she thinks. Jane is right. An agent appreciates someone who shows interest and spends time preparing for a meeting. As long as the interviewee doesn't act desperate she is off to a good start.

Jane feels nervous. Because she knows how important it is to be on time, she leaves home early. Besides, she doesn't know the roads yet and expects to encounter heavy traffic. She stays off her cell phone and focuses her thoughts on the interview. How great it would be if she could land an agent right away!

Back in the apartment, Dick wishes he had an appointment too. Not to worry, there is a ball game on TV.

Jane parks at a meter a few blocks from the agent's office. She is thirty minutes early. Although there is enough time to check herself over, think about the upcoming meeting and take some deep breaths, a feeling of fear is taking over. She needs to make a good impression. She needs some kind of a trick or technique to overcome that appearance of nervousness so she will seem relaxed and confident. Jane remembers what a wise man once told her:

*Fake it till you make it.*

Yes, actually pretend to be confident. Before you walk into that room, plan on acting like a person that is strong and comfortable with yourself. Then, enter the room and act strong and comfortable.

Does that seem difficult to do or unrealistic? I wouldn't be surprised if you felt that way. It's one thing to go through years of therapy and work on becoming a confident person who feels comfortable with oneself. But, if you are not already confident and comfortable, remember that as an actor, you want to take advantage of a current opportunity. You can't wait to feel better about yourself. You have to do it *now*. You don't want to miss what could amount to be the opportunity of a lifetime. So, fake it!

And you don't have to wait for an audition or interview to pretend to have confidence. Practice at everyday events. When you say hello to someone, say it with gusto. When you return unsatisfactory merchandise and the clerk doesn't seem to care about your situation, speak up and be firm. So, even if you don't feel a certain way, act it! Remember, you're an actor. And if you're not, you can employ this same technique.

Once you start acting this way it gets incorporated into your system. You will see how valuable this technique can be. The fact is you don't have time to wait in order to develop a feeling of comfort (if you don't already have one). Meetings and auditions must be taken advantage of now, not five years into your career.

## Is That Agent
## Right For Me

Dick sits at home waiting for Jane to return. He has been thinking about Jane's meeting with the agent and wishes he were in her place. It's been almost three hours since Jane left the apartment and he wonders if the time was filled with negotiating traffic or the meeting itself. (It was both).

The door opens. Dick detects a smile on Jane's face. It went well. Did the agent at New Talent tell her that he wants to "sign her"? Well, there were two agents in the room. The lady seemed to like Jane and her tenacity. The guy was also from New York and related to Jane. The meeting was lively and lasted an hour. They discussed her training and theatre credits. Jane politely asked the agents some well thought out questions such as the make-up of their clientele. They all viewed her composite tape. The agents discussed her picture. They liked it but thought that she could take a better one. They felt that it was a little stiff and could be more natural. Perhaps in color? Perhaps outdoors as opposed to a N.Y. studio? So, does it seem likely that Jane will be asked to be a client? Often, the last words said in a meeting are telling. In this case, they told Jane that she was a talented actor, that they didn't have anyone in her category, and that they would let her know of their decision in the morning.

The morning passed. It is 1 PM and still no call. Jane thinks that things are looking bleak. Even if they were going to call, it now seems that it probably won't be till after lunchtime. But they said that they would call in the morning. It becomes 3 PM and Dick says that they should get out of the apartment and go down the street for some coffee at the neighborhood Coffee Bean. Jane wants to wait. A little lesson here: when someone says he's going to call at a certain time or, say, that you'll find out if you got a particular job by Friday, don't take the person literally. His intentions may be good but everyday things often get in the way. There is no reason to waste time and energy worrying excessively and thinking negative thoughts.

The phone rings around 4:30. It is the agents on a conference call to Jane. Good news. They tell Jane that she is welcome at their agency. Rather than requesting an immediate decision from Jane, they wisely tell her to think about it and call them the next day. When Dick hears this he tells Jane to make them wait a few days.

"Let's look into this," Dick says. "They seem too small."

"The agents said that they run a boutique agency," Jane says. "They handle a manageable amount of clients and that allows them to attend to a client's needs."

"What about the big agencies like William Morris, ICM, CAA, UTA, Endeavor?"

That makes Jane think. She needs time to go up the hill to fetch a pail of water and think it over. She likes the smaller agency. They seem nurturing.

Knowledgeable. They told her of their success with current and past clients. She was flattered by being told they really wanted her.

What to do? That's easy to answer. Don't walk, *run* to the smaller agency. Why? It's not as though the bigger agencies are interested in meeting her or signing her. She tried to meet with them. She sent her picture and resume with a well-written cover letter. She followed up with phone calls. All to no avail. And besides, the bulk of auditions for both small and substantial roles on pilots, series and movies come from the lesser-known agencies. The bigger agencies might not have the desire or incentive to procure auditions or work for newer actors because there is relatively little money in it for them to do so. It is the smaller agencies that do the difficult work of getting their clients auditions for most of the roles in TV pilots and series regular roles and feature films. Although there are times when it may be advantageous to be with the very large agencies, this is not one of them. Fortunately, Jane recognizes that at a bigger agency the chances of getting "lost" and never receiving proper representation increase. You, Dick and Jane are too valuable to allow that to happen.

So how does it ordinarily work? The big agencies prefer to sign you after you have become a series regular or have a big movie coming out. When that time comes they can be persistent. When they want someone, they go for it; the sky's the limit. Scripts sent to you everyday, flowers, gifts, lunches, dinners, limos, and much more. All to convince you that they can treat you the way you deserve, and that they are more aware of which important roles and projects are available than your current agent is. And, that they can deliver those opportunities to you and get you those jobs.

Beware.

This is the mentality of some of the bigger agencies: sign anybody whose phone is currently ringing or who is likely to soon be in demand. The strategy is to sign a client when things are already happening rather than representing someone from the beginning, thereby taking advantage of a smaller agency's hard work.

In spite of this, there are times when it is wise for

an actor to "move on." Although the agent might be a "Johnny come lately," there are some occasions when switching agents is appropriate such as when your original agency cannot provide you with important job opportunities. For example, a larger agency may set up an appointment for you with a prolific director or writer, particularly if they represent him or her. The fact is: you are number one and have to watch out for yourself. Leaving an agent who believed in you in the beginning may be uncomfortable for you, but it may be the necessary thing to do. Just make sure that you have given enough consideration to any agency changes. Being wined and dined doesn't cut it.

Let's look at the reasons why staying with the agent who brought you to the dance is usually the smarter choice. That's easy. They have known you for a long period of time, they probably like you, know your talents and know what makes you tick. They know which casting people know and like you and which don't (all very valuable information that is needed to get you auditions that will further your career). There's something to be said for what's already working. The expression "don't fix it if it ain't broken" is appropriate here.

Additionally, when an agent who is employed by (or is a partner of) a large agency signs someone he may receive a stream of payments or bonuses based on the client's continued success. As a result, an agent may "push" the clients that he "signed" (brought into the agency) to the near exclusion of the agency's other clients. He is part of a corporate environment and seeks to climb the corporate ladder. This means that you may not get the attention of the other agents at the company. You may not even get the continued attention of the one who signed you (known as your "responsible agent"). And if your agent's phone is not ringing with offers for your services, your responsible agent will invariably tell you that it would be better for you if you moved on to a different agency. They may even say, "We don't want to hold you back." What B.S. The fact is they no longer want to work on your career when they realize that the momentum built up before you got there no longer exists. That momentum probably would have continued if the actor had stayed with the previous agent who got him to that point in his or her career.

I will never forget something similar that happened to me. I started managing a new client who had never done any professional work. In fact, she wasn't even in SAG. Working with her on all aspects of her career included placing her with a theatrical agent, which I did. About six months later she was cast in an NBC one-hour drama pilot for a new series. A week into shooting she told me that an agent at William Morris came down to the set and told her she was great and wanted to sign her. I was pleased that she told me about what happened and I immediately started looking into the situation. Only a few days later, my client called me and told me that all of the actors on the pilot were approached by that agent professing similar admiration for them and offering to sign all of them! It turns out that agent wanted to sign anybody he could get a hold of associated with that particular pilot. While the bigger agency does hope for continued success for a newly signed client in other projects or in renegotiating an actor's current series contract, one of the primary goals of a large agency is to seek control of as many of the elements of a series as possible. In this way, when a job becomes available, the agency representing several of the key players of the series (for example, having previously signed an actor, a producer, and an executive producer on the series) now has the power to influence the decision to hire one of his other clients for this new job. That's how it often works in Hollywood.

The lesson here is to give serious consideration to someone who wants to meet with you (provided it seems their intentions are honorable). You have nothing to lose by granting an interview. Sometimes it takes energy to do something that doesn't seem ideal. While Dick would have passed on Jane's meeting because he thinks a big agency is the only way to go, in the business of pursuing work, you must explore all opportunities. A small agent who is not your first choice, upon examination, may be exactly what's needed in your career situation. Realize that a small sized agency may be an able agency, and it may be hungry and, therefore, fight harder for you. The agents may be pros but with a less fashionable address. And a pro knows what sells. Remember, most of the actors who are movie stars or series regulars on TV today were not developed by the larger agents. Rather, they were developed by a small agency, one that put the actor's career on the right path and then painstakingly worked for success.

Now, back to Dick and Jane. He is marching around the apartment saying that the agency that Jane is considering is not powerful enough, that "they don't represent any stars." But, Jane must have read these last few pages because she decides to go with New Talent!

# Time To Audition

Jane lies on her bed thinking happy thoughts. She has an agent. With that knowledge comes a sense of relief. She feels that a big milestone in her journey has been reached and that there will now be professional support in her quest.

Her mind drifts back to her ten-year-old birthday party. The party guests are in the midst of devouring the cake and nobody seems to be paying attention to her. But then, her mother asks her to get up and sing a song for the guests. It takes Jane about a second to think about the unexpected request. She gets up, finds a good spot where everybody can see her, and starts wailing. She isn't very good but that is the moment that Jane decides to become an actress. She loves the attention and she loves the applause.

Whether you're an actor, someone "behind the camera," manager, agent, accountant, lawyer, or studio executive, each career starts differently. For Jane, it was her mother's prompting. For you, it may be schooling, a mentor, a summer job, an overwhelming desire for recognition. Whatever it was it lead to a desire to become an actor even though many people might have tried to discourage you. Don't let them. Fight for what you want. Feel confident. Does it matter what others think? No, it only matters what you think. Whether or not you are correct about your career choice or the way in which you pursue it, it is you who needs to make the mistakes (which are usually opportunities in disguise anyway). Besides, how many "accomplished" people ended up doing something they originally pursued? A lawyer ends up owning and operating a McDonald's franchise. An actor becomes a governor or president. A video store employee ends up owning a DVD distribution and production company. A busboy becomes the owner of the restaurant. A policeman guarding a movie set ends up in acting.

And where is Dick in all of this? Well, during his last year of college, Dick joined two buddies at a Mets game. One of them was studying to become a stockbroker and the other was a working actor. In fact, his actor friend was a regular player on the New York based soap opera "All My Children." He was making good money on a weekly basis. He was written about in magazines and his name sometimes appeared in gossip columns. And the girls definitely took notice when his friend entered a room. This was all too much for Dick. He loved this acting thing. Money, fame and girls!

Fortunately for Dick, he had a good look and some talent. His friend recommended him as an extra on the show and he was cast as a patron in a school cafeteria scene. Dick was hired for three days of work as a background player. His job was to eat lunch at a table alongside a table of the soap's regular players. All seemed to go well the first day and Dick was beaming. The light faded when he was told that the show's producer wanted to talk to him. After all, he was only an extra and producers and directors hardly ever speak with background players. He wondered if he did something wrong. He timidly walked over to the director's office. "Yes sir," said Dick. "Nice work today, your facial expressions were in sync with the scene's action. I'm giving you a line to say for tomorrow's show." And so, Dick's career shifted into high gear, at least in Dick's mind.

For Dick, a friend's help led to his first job. Although Dick did get some acting training in New York, his path to becoming a solid working actor would be filled with obstacles and require a great deal of effort and work. But before we move on to Jane's first audition, let's take a closer look at why Dick's apparent good fortune as a result of his friend's help might be harmful to pursuing acting in the long run.

When something fortuitous happens in one's career it might taint one's understanding of how it may work in the future. Take a politician. The first time he runs for election it is in a district that heavily favors his political party. He wins and ends up believing that getting elected is relatively easy. A pretty girl applies for a waitress job without any references or waitressing background. Fortunately for her, the lonely manager hires her on the spot. When her boss' advances are rejected, she is fired and finds that getting her next waitressing job is not so easy to come by. Both the politician's and the waitress' experiences are similar to Dick's. They were deluded into thinking that the road to success involved little effort. So, although Dick's attitude was influenced by what happened to him early in his career, hopefully he soon learns that luck (which is great to have) has a short shelf life.

As we root for Dick to change his approach to his career, Jane awaits her first audition. Until then, Jane has been going to acting classes regularly, in basic technique, scene study and cold reading. She's made an appointment with a photographer for new pictures. She reworked her resume to make it more LA friendly (placing film and TV credits above theatre, and removing "has driver's license" in the miscellaneous category as one would do in New York City). She looked through her wardrobe to make certain that she had appropriate things to wear for upcoming auditions. She watched the new TV programs and went to movies when she had time. And she made a list of everyone that she has met in the acting business with their contact information and the circumstances under which they met. Whew. Jane is a worker and will likely benefit by it in a big way.

The phone rings. A call from her agency. It's not the agent who signed her or even one of the other agents at the firm. Rather, it's an assistant (who is probably working his or her way up to becoming an agent) calling Jane with information regarding an appointment. Jane finds the assistant to be friendly but he seems rushed. He gives Jane the name of the show, the role and brief description of the character, the time, day and location of the audition, who she will be auditioning for, and faxes her the "sides" (the pages from the script that the actor will audition from). Time of phone call: under three minutes.

Dick is on the couch watching TV when he hears the fax machine churning out paper. He stops munching on the potato chips, puts down the can of beer, approaches the machine, and looks over the incoming sides. "Looks like there's a role here for me, too," he calls out to Jane. Although it is Jane's audition, she wants to help Dick and suggests that they rehearse the sides together.

After a few minutes working on the sides, Dick stops to ask Jane if she is going to audition with the casting director alone or will the director be there also. Jane says it is for the casting director only.

"Are you serious?" says Dick. "That's a waste of time. You have to eventually audition for the director anyway in order to get the job. Might as well have the director there. So, tell your agent that you want to read for the director, too."

That may sound logical, but it doesn't work like that when you're new and, not necessarily when you're a veteran either. (In many instances, you should be satisfied getting the audition.) It's more important that the casting director believes that you're right for the role and then helps you get it. Before your audition with the producer or director, the casting director might tell you what they are looking for. He or she may tell you how they want to see the role played (show more sadness when saying a particular line, don't act as angry, and so on). Information like this could get you the job. Also, producers and directors have high regard for the casting director, who is hired for her expertise. They want that person (who may be paid tens of thousands of dollars) to select the best candidates for the role thereby finding them a great cast and saving them valuable pre-production time.

On the day of the audition, Dick drives Jane to the meeting. They find street parking outside of Paramount Studios (they are not allowed to park on the lot) and walk through the gates to the audition. Impressive place. There are old and new studio buildings, a few cars that were given permission to drive on the lot, important looking people mulling about, and in the distance they can see a windowless wall that is painted to look like blue sky (obviously used as a movie backdrop). Jane is in awe and starts getting nervous. Dick notices the commissary (where important people sometimes eat) and wants to check it out, have some coffee there, and get discovered.

Jane finds the room where the audition is taking place. She signs in and sits down among the other actresses there to read for the part. Although she feels prepared to read the sides, she notices that the other actresses are dressed casually as if they are at home. The role was of a lawyer and Jane was the only one there dressed as though she could be in court trying a case. Had the assistant at the agency not given Jane the correct information? He did seem in a hurry when they spoke. (What I'm getting at here is an aspect of Jane's relationship with her agency and whether she would benefit by having a manager, a subject that will be explored as we follow Jane's journey.)

Something else bothers Jane even more. In looking around the room, all the other actresses appear right for the role. Jane clearly recognizes one of them who was the star of a TV series that was on the air the previous season. This girl was well known! Jane's impulse is to get up and leave. She wonders how she is going to get the role when she is up against a recognizable and well-known person?

The answer is simple. If the recognizable actress

was such a sure bet to get the role, she would have already been offered it (and not have had to come in to audition for it). Actually, Jane virtually has the same chance to get the role as the actress from the series. In fact, she might even have a better chance because this audition is for an attorney as opposed to the sweet airhead that the actress played on her series. Possibly an agent or manager was trying to have their client seen for a different kind of role than she was already known for and as a result, an audition was required by the director. In other words, Jane should not be intimidated. Nor should you in the same situation.

Once you are in that room auditioning for the role, you will be receiving serious consideration. The playing field has leveled out. It is up to you at that point. Do a good job and you will win the role or at least, be called in again for a future part. Additionally, expect your agent to get good feedback from the casting director. What we have here is an opportunity that an actor can take advantage of as opposed to a situation to be fearful of. If you are fearful, you know what to do! Fake it till you make it!

Jane does an adequate job at the audition, good enough for the casting director to tell the agent that she will "bring her in" for a future role. Too bad that this is something that Jane doesn't learn about for a few days because she leaves the office feeling dejected and remains that way all day.

One of the other actresses from the audition notices her pout. "Don't feel you did too well, huh?"

Jane nods and says that she figured the competition would be huge but the real problem is that she doesn't feel that she got all the information from the agency's assistant. This new actress friend tells Jane that the agents don't necessarily call with the audition appointment because they're too busy with casting directors securing other auditions. "I've got a manager who deals with the agency and a great deal of other things, too," she says. Jane also learns that a preponderance of actors have managers these days. Twenty years ago it was a handful, and they barely existed in the '60's. She wonders if it is significant that actors have managers in greater numbers than ever before.

Jane wants to hear more about managers and they decide to have coffee in the commissary.

This makes Dick very happy.

# Lots Of Representatives

Jane's inquisitiveness about managers elicits some questions. She asks her new friend from the audition if she thinks that she needs one; what they do; what it will cost her. Jane likes what she hears. She figures that if this "advice and guidance" thing that managers do actually pans out, that they may be worth another ten to fifteen percent in addition to the agent's ten percent commission.

"No way, that's nuts" said Dick. "You're lookin' at giving away twenty-five percent of what you make."

Jane thinks about that but believes that, provided she can get a good manager, seventy-five or eighty percent of something is better than one hundred percent of nothing. Smart thinking, Jane.

Note: Before we continue discussing managers, be aware that the commission paid to a manager, as with an agent and other business expenses of an actor (pictures, tapes, acting classes, wardrobe for a role and so on), is tax deductible. So, for example, if you're making decent money, a ten percent commission paid to a manager is closer to five percent when you compute the taxes that one pays.

Jane learns that knowledgeable managers do a lot of things. They put you with an agent who is right for you. They make sure that the agent gets appointments for you in the first place, remind the agent of your existence and of your many attributes and credits. He might say, "Don't forget, she sings and that's what the role calls for," "He's tall and previously played the role of a basketball player in a TV episode so why not in that movie," or "The film is being directed by the same director he worked for in a project last season." Sometimes the manager will tell the agent of a new project being cast. If a manager had been involved in Jane's last audition situation he would have been the person who received the audition information from the assistant directly and then, because he probably has only a handful of clients, he would have had the time to fully discuss with Jane not only the vital data of an audition but also the ins and outs of how to get the job. Sometimes, a manager "plays agent" and gets you auditions on his own, something that is not only beneficial to you but helps your agent too. Presumably, a manager knows many casting directors and producers. What else from a manager? He supervises the deal making process assuring the best deal under the circumstances occasionally employing the technique known as "good cop/bad cop." During the process, he tries to keep egos of representatives and others in check so as to prevent deals from going south thereby preventing the loss of a job and opportunity for growth. Also, he or she often speaks with producers, executives, directors and others connected with a production that you are working on in order to keep things running smoothly. A manager may play psychologist to you. He or she is aware of publicity and promotion needs, and might be aware of tax breaks and of the law.

What about the essential every day tools that an

actor uses? A manager gives advice concerning your pictures, resume, bio, and composite tape (the "reel.") These items change regularly and must be attended to with the help of the manager.

What about considerations concerning your physical appearance? A manager will likely discuss appropriate audition attire, hair, makeup, and many other items related to your "look." And what about your body? Ah, your body. Unless you are a character actor, did you ever notice how the industry is casting women and men these days? Invariably, they are in good shape. So, it is *your* job to be in good shape. It is not good enough for the actor or actress to say "if I get the job, I'll lose the weight before filming begins." A producer or director wants to see what he's getting on the spot. He or she doesn't want to guess what you will look like when shooting begins or on the day they are taping the show. Think of it this way: putting off caring for your body is similar to the person who says, "If I get a date, I'll lose the extra pounds." As an actor you're in front of the camera so act accordingly.

As Jane learns of the manager's many duties

she begins to understand how a manager could be valuable to her career. The difference between an agent and manager starts becoming clear. Besides the various functions of each, she realizes it even more fully when she considers the following: since an agency represents scores of clients and a manager only represents a handful of clients, it is logical to assume that a manager must do something other than just hand-holding (which is also in the job description). She is right, of course. The manager does do a whole lot more. He or she is on top of the pyramid, so to speak, supervising all of the activities of an actor's career.

When Jane talks to her agency about getting a manager, some agents at New Talent balk and other agents think it is a good idea. Some agents worry that the manager will put the client with a different agency, but others are pleased to have a manager present to take care of and look out for the client.

How do you find a manager? Ask your friends, colleagues in class, your acting teachers, look at lists of managers and send submission packages (picture and resume) to them by standard mail or by email. If you are represented by an agency, ask the agents there. This last method needs some critical thought. Let's say that your agent often works with a particular manager and together they "share" clients. In that case, there may be some loyalty between them so that they refer clients to each other regularly. Sometimes there may be a feeling that one "owes" the other after having previously referred a valuable client. So, you have to ask yourself, should I go to that particular manager where I am in a "payback" situation and the agent feels obligated to the manager because of having been sent a client previously? Or, will being represented by such a manager be more productive because the agent and manager have a strong working relationship and even a friendship that will be beneficial to me? Of course, although the latter is usually better, there may be a combination of factors that control the relationship. In entertainment, you will find that there are really no "clean" and impartial relationships. Most every aspect concerning the business of acting is overlapping. Conflicts of interest exist. Fighting them is probably futile but know they exist and deal with them. There is no reason to think that other businesses and politics are any different.

A final word. It is usually preferable to secure a manager first. The overriding reason is that a good manager knows which agents are out there, what kind of clients they work with effectively (for example, beginning and/or established actors), and whether as a manager he has a strong working relationship with the agency. He can help you find an agent right for you. In this way, your team of supporters takes shape. You will, therefore, prosper more effectively.

When you have your "team" together, and each member of the team performs their function well, your chances of success are greatly improved. A team may include not only the agent and manager but also a commercial agent (for TV, radio commercials and print ads), although some agencies represent actors for both theatrical and commercial employment, and

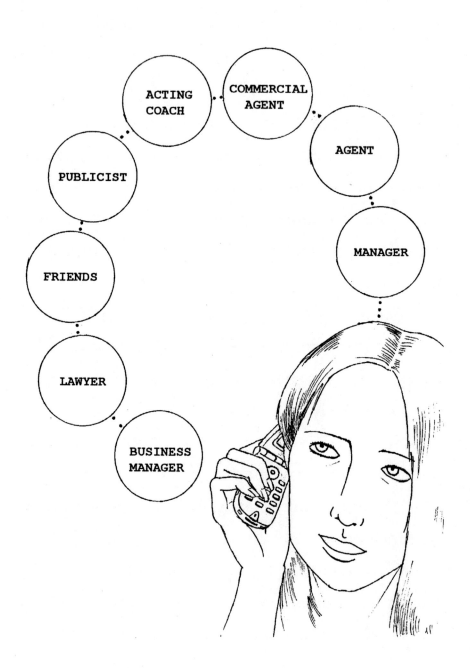

any one or more of the following: a publicist, lawyer, business manager, your acting teacher, acting coach, your mentor, your spouse or significant other, your friends.

Later that evening, Dick grudgingly goes with Jane to a showcase. A showcase is a theatrical event where actors perform scenes on stage to an audience that may include casting directors, agents and managers but more often is populated by friends of the performers. Dick wants to see a movie but agrees to support a friend by going.

After the performances, they go to a coffeehouse and discuss the showcase and the value of having a "team."

They all feel that a beginning actor or an actor with a few credits doesn't need a huge "team" around them; it seems that an agent and manager would suffice. It bothers Dick to think that so many others would be involved in his career. Even if Dick understood that a large team is necessary when he is working all the time, the real problem is that Dick isn't the type to ask for help. He avoids asking for directions when he is lost. He likes being self-reliant. He wants to handle things as opposed to taking advice from others, even from a knowledgeable manager. (Actually, Dick would prefer things to just happen...the thought of being discovered at a luncheonette counter is Dick's fantasy. Psychologists call it "magical thinking." In acting and in business, asking and taking advice is necessary.)

One must be open to asking for help. If you sit back and "think" about reaching out, you may be left out. The fact is you have nothing to lose. Every small or large request that one makes in acting could help in the process of achieving success. You never know. A door could open for you. It might actually be the door to success. Even if you don't receive an answer that you consider satisfactory, the act of asking is a positive step. It could trigger an answer that makes you think about a new way of doing something. Like rehearsing, the act of asking is invigorating. The only caveat is to ask appropriate people such as your friends, teacher, manager and only on rare occasions your agent. Remember an agent has many clients and prefers to spend time seeking auditions for them, not answering questions. There was a time when managers were rare and the agent welcomed questions and consultations on every subject but that was when agents were not under today's industry pressure to earn money and compete viciously with their fellow agents. The agent, who is essential to one's acting career, works on volume these days. For agents the mantra is likely "book, book, and book more." (Not that a manager is immune to this thinking although for him your long-term career goals are paramount.)

# Climbing The Ladder

Jane is climbing the steps of her career ladder but Dick hasn't yet gotten a foothold. Jane has found an agent and has been exploring constructive ways to become a working actor. Dick is negative or is not motivated. The other night the duo was talking after watching a movie starring Charlie Sheen. Dick talked about Sheen's having become a star "because of his family heritage, his father Martin Sheen and all." Time to stop right there!

One of the most important concepts in pursuing acting and being successful is to realize that it does *not* matter if you don't know someone in the business. I was once a member of a panel at a seminar where the person next to me was a well-known publicist. He asked the audience of actors to raise their hand if they thought that it was necessary to know someone important in order to make it. Nearly all of the two hundred actors in the audience raised their hand. The publicist was about to continue when I grabbed the microphone and said, to their surprise, that such belief was untrue. Whoa, did I get one of those looks from the publicist along with a puzzled look from the audience.

Although logic demands that knowing someone can be very helpful (it certainly can't hurt), the fact is that of all the stars and successful working actors in the business, very few of them knew anybody when they started. Sure, there are some show biz families such as the Sheens, Baldwins, and Douglases, but the vast majority of stars today didn't know anybody that could be of real help to them in the early stages of their career. You make it by following the basic steps to success: acting training, attitude, representation and perseverance.

To illustrate the point further, consider all the

actors in movies and TV series. Notice that the overwhelming majority was without a show biz namesake and that they came to town with nothing but talent and fortitude. I see pilots and new series every season that are cast with unknowns. The same holds true with movies where many actors do small independent films and get discovered when their film does well. A star or "hot" actor can emerge from only one scene in a movie. In fact, a sought after actor can come from a TV commercial! A film or TV casting director (or a director or producer) may be watching television and notice someone in a commercial and request that person come in and audition for a part in her project .

Let's take an example of how it often works and how it can work for you. You're an actor and your agent is getting you auditions (or you are getting the auditions for yourself). You land a couple of small jobs and start being seen for guest starring roles in episodes of series. You then audition for a pilot for a TV series. It sells and the network puts the series on the air. Lo and behold, you're on a series! Now you are the series regular. You didn't know anybody in the beginning. Rather, you made the right steps, talent met opportunity, and everybody now asks you how you magically did it (but you know how you did it, you trained hard and pursued hard).

During the journey called your career, a journey you take without a road map, you should follow your heart and do what you feel is right. What's right is what's right for you. When you go after an agent, who's to say that sending submissions three times is wrong; some agents may be bothered and others may like your tenacity. When your manager negotiates for more money for the role for which you were just cast, who's to say that a call shouldn't be made to the business affairs department even if the casting director has said there is no more money. Ditto when a representative makes a call to the producer after the casting director says the actor is not right for the role or that the actor can't have special billing. Can a call hurt? If the answer is no, it's no. But perhaps it won't be. Who knows if being on a game show or reality show will act as your catapult? They have been the catalyst on some occasions.

Who knows if being on a soap opera will hurt or help your chances of doing a TV series or an important feature film? Certainly not. Look at Tom Selleck, Demi Moore, Meg Ryan, Alec Baldwin, Sarah Michelle Gellar and Lindsay Lohan who started in soaps. In general, actors and others in the business used to believe that doing television would hurt your chances or prevent you from doing feature films. Now, actors try to get on television (as a series regular) in order to become desirable in the movie world. They might perform on television in order to reactivate their feature careers. (Example: Glenn Close took a role on FX's "The Shield").

Things change with societal mores and with economic realities. Do what you believe is best for you. Any approach can work for you and take you further along in your career. No longer can anything hold you back. It's not a path that one would recommend, but even with her roots in pornography, Traci Lords went on to work in conventional projects.

There was a time when people in the industry said that the half-hour sitcoms were dead, that only drama shows would get good ratings. Then came the "Cosby" show, and actors, producers and networks wanted to be involved with sitcoms. When comedies were king, the industry said that one-hour dramas were dead and people shied away from dramas. Guess what happened? Dramas reemerged.

When it seemed unwise to program shows on Saturday night because ratings were so low in that "daypart," the networks considered abandoning that evening's programming to local markets. Then, along came the one-hour drama "Dr. Quinn, Medicine Woman." Ratings were up. Network programming on Saturday night was back.

When Friday night seemed a programming wasteland, "Miami Vice" proved otherwise. When it seemed that being a series cast member on the new network FOX was a waste of time compared to being on CBS, NBC or ABC, along came "21 Jump

Street" and the emergence of Johnny Depp! Similar to popular entertainment trends that are supposedly never ending, the same applies to trends in real estate and the stock market. When everybody believes that something will continue in a particular direction, that's when things reverse course.

In the early days, music videos were the rage and some actresses performing in them actually got discovered! In 1984, "Friends" alumna Courteney Cox's big break was her appearance in Bruce Springsteen's music video "Dancing In The Dark." As a result, actresses wanted to be cast in music videos even if the video wasn't done by a known group or singer. Agents and managers frequently heard, "I want to 'go up' for music videos" even from actresses who had previously scoffed at the idea of doing a music video because it was a new and different form of production where you didn't have lines to speak.

Take the example of Tom Hanks. He not only did a half-hour comedy series ("Bosom Buddies") but one that was considered a "T and A" (tits and ass) show. That didn't prevent him from being cast in the male lead in the feature film "Splash," and you know where his career has gone from there.

In other words, you never know where success will come from. Just about anything other than some criminal offenses could be your ticket to success. You never know. The moral here: in acting, *there are no rules.*

Think about it. There are no rules in life either. People from unconventional backgrounds with unpopular ideas can become successful.

How do Dick and Jane feel about this issue of pursuing without compunction?

Let's take a step back and find out what Jane did with the information she received about managers. After researching who was out there, Jane finds and signs with a manager. He is relatively unknown with a small clientele, has great enthusiasm for Jane's career and he is a hard worker. The manager wisely calls the casting director who had auditioned Jane for the guest-starring role on that series a few days earlier. As a new manager, he wants to introduce himself to the casting director but it is more important for him to talk about his new client. The phone call reminds her of what a good reading Jane did. She calls to discuss Jane with the show's producers. They trust her assessment and tell the casting director to offer Jane a particular one-line role in an upcoming episode that seems perfect for her.

Jane gets an offer for work!

Question for Dick and Jane: Is one line good enough? Dick thinks that one line is ridiculous since Jane had previously auditioned for a guest-starring role in the show and had done well. "Now, you should only be auditioning for other big roles in their series," he says. Good advice?

Jane thinks about what to do and calls her new manager.

"Sure you should do it," the manager says. "It's your first job out here. It will jump start things. Fire up the momentum. I can hype it and use it to help get you other things."

Dick tries again. "If you do a role in the series now it'll prevent you from doing a larger role in the series later in the season." What Dick says is true since a series rarely likes to use the same actor for different roles, but there are scores of other series to work on and doing this one will likely increase Jane's chances of getting work on other shows.

There are other reasons. Jane may be liked by the director and he or she may want to work with her in something else. Same for the casting director. Jane will get to meet people and be seen professionally by people who could be beneficial to her. By the time Jane is scheduled to work, the role might be rewritten giving her additional lines. Though one line may feel inconsequential, the role may recur in future episodes. (In this case, the role offered Jane is a police desk clerk. Clearly, in a show about cops at a police station where Jane's character works, the desk clerk character could be written into future episodes.) And, of course, Jane will make some money.

Don't hold yourself back. Don't be wary of doing small roles or untried projects. Don't have preconceptions. Consider that every successful actor out there has a different story about how he or she got started. *There are no rules.* Maybe the career began in a soap opera, a kids TV show, a one line role in an episode of a TV series, a commercial, a music video, a game show, a reality show, theatre, a tour guide at Universal Studios, business, police work, politics. In acting, after you finish your training, you don't go to a placement office and receive a choice of auditions and jobs. Therefore, the name of the game is getting things started, do your very best, and see where the train takes you.

I remember seeing Ted Danson doing a line or two in an episode of "Mork & Mindy" (a Paramount TV series) in which he played an effeminate hair stylist. It's possible that's how Paramount discovered him because he was later cast in another of the studio's TV series, "Cheers," as the lead! It's hard to argue that the very small role he did in the show hurt his career. Rather, it got him seen by decision makers who were thereby made aware of his talent. Raquel Welch started with three lines in an episode of "Bewitched." Teri Hatcher of "Desperate Housewives" proudly announces at award ceremonies that when she arrived in L.A. her first job was as a dancer on "The Love

Boat." So, *you never know. There are no rules.*

In my early days of managing careers, I watched movies on weekend afternoons, sometimes two a day. I wanted to learn what was out there. I also rented movies to catch up on important films that I had missed over the years. I rented "Fast Times At Ridgemont High" and thought that I saw Nicolas Cage in a high school cafeteria scene uttering but a couple of lines. In order to be certain it was he, I waited till the end of the film and watched the "crawl" (the long list of actors and their roles). I was right. And look where Cage is today. He did that small role even though he was the nephew of director Francis Ford Coppola (who could have opened any door for him).

Note: Watch movies and TV shows regularly. This keeps you fresh and aware of the trends. As for the trade publications such as *The Hollywood Reporter* and *Daily Variety,* I don't advise that you read them unless you are reading them for enjoyment because it is your job to pursue your career with your gut as opposed to concerning yourself with the intricacies of the business. Is it valuable to know how much a particular movie studio spent on marketing a film? No. But it is valuable for an actor to see the unconventional comedy, "There's Something About Mary." By studying others' performances, you'll understand your agent or manager when he says, "they're looking for the type of comedy found in the movie 'There's Something About Mary.' "

When pursuing a career outside of acting the same principle applies. Similar to taking a small role is taking a job that seems small or menial after having studied in school for years. For example, an English major in college seeks a glamorous job in the publishing industry. She continues her studies and earns a Masters Degree and a Doctorate. When it is time to look for that dream job in publishing, the student is offered a secretarial job in the marketing department of a publisher. A lot of schooling for nothing? No, a job that has fantastic opportunities for growth! (Dick wouldn't get it but Jane would relish the opportunity.)

Although a starting position seems unworthy, take advantage of any job where there may be growth potential. For example, a desk clerk at one of the hotels in a large chain, at an airline's ticket counter, a mailroom in a large company or nearly any starting position at a company that's in a growing industry. The point is, you never know where it could lead. Follow in the steps of industry titans that began their career in otherwise undesirable positions and moved up the ladder.

I graduated from law school with the hope that I could get into entertainment law. Jobs were few and far between. I offered to work for free at an entertainment law office in Manhattan (and I consider myself fortunate to have found a place that was receptive enough to even listen to my offer). I was hired, and even though I sometimes felt like a glorified secretary, I was ecstatic because I had embarked on my chosen career path and the journey had begun. Point of the story: have faith, perseverance and patience; make sacrifices if necessary (e.g. I offered my services for gratis), and don't forego your dreams because you can't have them today. Having a dream is the essence of building a career. But don't let that dreamy picture in your mind stop you from being practical about what you can do now. (Incidentally, when the attorney hired me he said that he didn't want me to work for free so he paid me $100 a week.)

# Social Time

Jane is rehearsing a scene for next Tuesday night's acting class with her scene partner. Like other actors without formal rehearsal rooms, they rehearse where they can. This time it was in Dick and Jane's apartment. They feel uncomfortable working in the living room because Dick is watching television there. So, they disappear into Jane's bedroom.

The scene they were working on came from a Neil Simon comedy. As you might imagine, the scene calls for a kiss. Jane's partner leans over for his smooch. Although the scene continues without a hitch, her partner kind of felt something (particularly when he bit his lip.)

Later that evening, Jane is asked by the acting scene partner if she wants to go to a party on Saturday night. The party will be attended by celebrities and people from the industry. Jane is no wallflower and wants to have some fun after a long week. She also thinks she might meet a person who could further her career. But, this presents a couple of problems for her. She considers Dick and wants him to have the opportunity of coming along with them since she believes it could be helpful to him career-wise. Secondly, she senses that her scene study partner is interested in her and she does not want to date at this time. And a third unforeseen problem will soon present itself at this "industry" party.

Jane's acting scene partner says Dick can come, too.

On Saturday night both Dick and Jane prepare themselves to go to the party. Jane's scene partner arrives promptly and announces himself on the building's intercom. Dick buzzes him in and greets him at the door with a "how you doin" pat on the back. Jane's scene partner understands the sudden warmth is because he agreed to let Dick come along.

As they drive to the party, Dick checks himself out in the car's vanity mirror. He looks as good as he could. "Wait' 'til I meet those producers, I'll rock 'em," he says. "After I talk about acting with them I'll tell them about my story idea for a movie."

Jane listens to this and isn't quite sure that Dick has the right idea for a party. Her scene partner, who has gone to many industry parties, rolls his eyes.

Yes, Dick is headed into a stonewall. But, Jane is also running into an issue. When actors and actresses without significant credits go to an industry party or event in order to "meet" someone that can further their career, they may face a dilemma. If you are talking with an industry type person there and blatantly assert that you are an actor, he or she will invariably ask you what projects you have been in and what you are doing now. Jane ran into just that situation once. It went like this: "So Jane, what have you done?"

Jane, feeling defensive, stammers a bit and says,

"Well, did some work in New York, a few days on a soap."

Although the industry person might find her honesty refreshing or he might be interested in Jane for personal reasons (as so often happens at these parties), chances are that Jane's career will not be helped by this exchange. Rather, that person, who is there with his wife or partner and expects to speak with others at his level, will move on to the next guest.

At industry gatherings, actors, young and old, are exposed to the usual Hollywood attitudes revolving around who you are and what have you done. To make the issue murkier, whether you are female or male, you may run up against unwanted advances. A word about advances: they may be difficult to differentiate from an interest in your acting potential. You may be asked for your phone number. If you are unsure of the person's intentions but are interested professionally, give the person a business card with your headshot (picture) and voicemail number. Someone may hand

you a business card so you can call the person the next day regarding a "project that you're so right for." If you are lucky, you will go home with enough business cards to paper your bathroom.

What is the best way for an actor to handle contacts at a Hollywood party or, for that matter, for any civilian who attends a party with business folks present? Answer: Just go to the party to have fun! Don't look for work there. If serious business should come out of it, so much the better. Chances are, the pressure to impress will lessen. The right attitude and results will follow. Consider this: people tend to warm up to actors (and others) who don't appear to have an agenda.

So, how does our group fare at the party? Well, Dick gets a couple of phone numbers, Jane fails to impress anyone, and her scene partner gets jealous.

# Back To Business

Our heroes are feeling good. Although Jane didn't promote her career at the party, she considers the party a positive learning experience, one of many she expects to have. Dick "scores" later in the week.

Pursuing acting is somewhat of a waiting game. During the week, Jane has to attend her acting classes. She rehearses scenes with a partner for their upcoming class. She has a manager and agent and occasionally goes to auditions. Still, she isn't comfortable having time on her hands. So, she thinks about what else she could do professionally. She thinks about doing a play that would not only enhance her resume but also give her a chance to be seen by an audience with some industry people including casting directors. But, getting cast in a local Equity Waiver play (limited to 99 seats and no pay for actors), particularly an entertaining one that would attract an "industry" audience, can take time to find. So while Jane looks for a play, she decides to be in a showcase.

Jane learns that a showcase can avail you the opportunity to perform on stage doing a scene (either with a partner or a monologue) in front of people that can further your career. She finds a new partner and a scene that they believe to be entertaining. They then search for an organization that puts on showcases. The one that they decide upon seems to have high standards, meaning that they have a track record for putting on quality showcases. It is well organized, well promoted, has a history for being seen by industry professionals, is performed in a venue that is accessible, and a reasonable fee is charged the actors (a few hundred dollars).

Dick isn't interested in performing for free in Equity Waiver theatre or paying to perform at a showcase. Jane is moving full speed ahead. In fact, her scene is well rehearsed, entertaining and funny, and receives hearty applause. A casting director who was looking for a new face for a TV pilot is in the audience! Sure enough, he approaches Jane and asks who her agent is. Nervously, Jane gives him the information and mentions that her manager is at the showcase, too. The casting director immediately speaks to Jane's manager and sets up an audition for the half-hour sitcom pilot.

Jane studies hard before the audition. She even does the audition scene in her acting class. She goes to an acting coach to give her insight into performing the material and interpreting the script and her character. She discusses the role with her manager. On the way to the beach to recover from the anxiety, she stops into a boutique to buy an outfit that perfectly suits the character.

Jane goes to the audition early. She signs in. Takes a seat. She sees recognizable actresses sitting around the room waiting to audition for the same role as Jane's. She has learned that she has as much chance to get the role as they do. However, she isn't prepared for what the casting director does next. He comes out of his office and gives a big hug to one of the auditioning actresses exclaiming he is so glad that she could make it to the audition. At first, Jane's heart sinks. After all the work she has done, now this. What if that actor has an inside track? But no, Jane decides that she will not let this faze her. She says to herself "fake it till you make it," and she proceeds to act like her presence is as valuable as anybody else's. Do you know what happened? She faked it and made it – in the waiting room, and in the audition room where the writer, director, producers, studio executives and casting director watched. She got through the audition with flying colors. But, it wasn't over yet. She still has to undergo a network "test" (a final audition in front of all of the people who saw her at the earlier audition plus the network executives; additionally, a pilot and series deal have to be pre-negotiated by the agent and producers in the event Jane is chosen).

Whew. Jane finds herself preparing again for the following week's meeting. She meets with both her

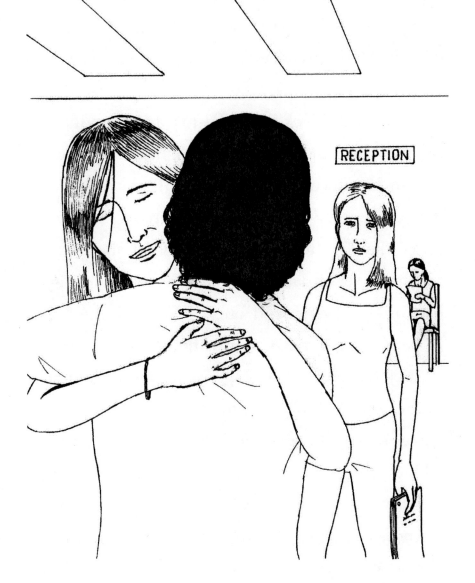

manager and her agent over breakfast. Can Jane pull it out? She learns that the network executives want a name or recognizable face for the role. Fortunately, the casting director and the show's creator want her (although the network usually makes the final decision with a TV pilot).

Meanwhile, Dick has been told by a producer at another party that he was very right for a particular role in his upcoming series. (Unlike a pilot for a possible series, Dick is being considered for a network series that is already sold for at least six episodes and has a set airdate.) Boy, is he happy. "This is it", he thinks. "My friend on 'All My Children' back in New York is not going to believe this. Whoa."

Dick tells everyone. A good agent shows interest in him but Dick blows him off because he thinks a bigger one will come after him. He does the same with a struggling actor friend and breaks a date with a girl who he thinks is a hanger-on. These people are now a waste of his time; he is about to be with people at a higher level. He says to Jane, "Let's get some dinner to discuss our stuff. I especially want to go over your career." Jane stares incredulously at him, and declines to join him. Even if Dick wasn't acting so obnoxiously, she wants to rehearse for her pilot and get her rest.

Dick goes out by himself for a drink and runs into an actor he knows. The actor tells Dick that he has had enough of the business and he is getting into real estate. He is going to study for his license. "Say what? Are you nuts," Dick says. "The opportunities that you have in acting, the money, the parties, how can you walk away from that? And besides, I'm getting a series. I'll help you."

Meanwhile, Jane's manager calls and writes the network to promote his client. He sends an attractive package to the producers that includes Jane's picture, resume, composite tape, N.Y. theatre press clippings and an enticing cover letter. The manager thinks: "Whatever it takes; getting the pilot will establish my client." The odds are against Jane but that doesn't stop him. The agency is also doing its job. It lobbies the network and casting director.

Jane sees what her agent and manager are doing

for her. They go the extra mile for her, something that happens daily – but actors don't hear about. Although the network hasn't made its decision yet, Jane calls her agent and manager to thank them for their efforts. Bingo! Doing what Jane did is of utmost importance in this business. Why? Because saying thank you, showing appreciation, is an extremely important gesture to a representative. It is something that most actors (and others in businesses everywhere) rarely do. Usually, they take help for granted. The mere expression of gratitude can be worth nearly as much to an agent or manager as the money they make from you. Yes, representatives need money to put bread on the table, but a word of appreciation can go a long way in terms of how hard the representative works for you in the future. In fact, it can be so effective that you might consider it a trick!

Note: Jane's way of saying thank you was special. She wrote a letter though she could have sent an email. Why is that significant? Because, unlike in the early days of the Internet when receiving an email was special and different, today it is special and different to receive a letter! (This is particularly true considering the abundance of emails received by busy people and the fact that emails are deleted, both intentionally and unintentionally). This concept of communicating by traditional letter writing applies to any business that is accustomed to depending on the Internet. So, if you want to get another person's attention, use a letter or note.

Dick is spending a lot of time waiting for the phone to ring lately. Unfortunately, he'll not get good news. He is getting too cocky and the producers feel it. During his auditions his acting isn't convincing and they worry that if his attitude is like this now, how is he going to behave on the set. (Note: They hire a guy for the role who looks something like Dick.)

Jane's wish is granted. Yes, she gets the job! She beats out her competition including the actresses that were recognizable names and faces. The producers and the network prefer Jane for a number of reasons: She looks right for the role they were casting, her attitude makes them feel that they and the cast could work well with her on the set, they feel she will handle publicity interviews and promotion well, her interpretation of the role is right on target, and the most important thing of all --Jane's audition is superb! *The bottom line for an actor is always talent!* Gone are the days when a look was all that matters.

# Dick and Jane
# Go Home

What separates Dick and Jane? In the near future the answer will be three thousand miles. Though, for now, I'm not referring to the physical distance between them but rather, their approach to the business. A Chinese proverb comes to mind that goes like this:

*Hungry man must wait long time*
*for roast duck to fly in mouth.*

Yes, it does seem that our buddy Dick wanted acting jobs and success to happen effortlessly. It's actually a virtue for him to be somewhat brash and confident in that it helps to have an element of assuredness in order to succeed. But, as you can see by Dick's methods (if you can call them that), his problem lies in his misunderstanding of what it takes to make it in acting. His problem is compounded by his sophomoric approach. Dick had gotten on the plane and expected to be whisked to success. Jane, on the other hand, used her wits and extensive efforts in pursuing her goal.

Let's get back to Dick and Jane's apartment and listen in to their discussion.

"I must say Jane, you did good. You succeeded in your mission. A pilot for a series, pretty cool."

Jane looks at him; she wants the same for Dick. "I'm lucky, I guess; I wish we were both doing the pilot."

Dick looks down and feels sad. Compared to Jane, he couldn't even get arrested. In reality, he knows he didn't put in the effort that Jane did. "Maybe I'll move back to New York and keep pursuing acting there," he says.

Actually, what is going through Dick's mind is real estate. He is thinking about the actor who said that he intended to get his real estate license. A job like that,

Dick thinks, calls for skills that I possess. It takes a people person and that's me.

Jane drives Dick to the airport. He is on his way back to New York. She parks the car and walks him into the terminal. Realizing that his flight was already boarding, he quickly reaches down to pick up his bags. Then he stops, drops his bags back onto the floor, turns toward Jane and gives her a hug. As Dick walks off he calls out: "Don't worry about me, I know every street in New York. I'll sell a million co-ops." He notices a pretty girl in tight jeans and follows along in her footsteps. Fortunately, she was walking towards his flight gate.

Jane gets back in the car. She thinks about Dick's being a real estate agent and wonders if he really has left acting for good or will try again in New York. She knows that, although she has moved from N.Y. and found success in L.A., an actor can still make it from anywhere. Jane is correct. While there is a difference in the number of opportunities between these two cities (and in the other cities where actors are often found pursuing their careers such as Minneapolis,

Chicago, Atlanta, Miami, Dallas, and San Francisco), the key to your success is to employ the methods that Jane used during her journey.

Jane drives back to her apartment in West Hollywood and pulls into her parking space. She turns off the ignition, sits back and sighs. She is home.

# MICHAEL J. WALLACH

has been a personal manager guiding the careers of actors and other industry professionals for more than 20 years. He also created and teaches a popular six-week course entitled "This Business of Acting™" for UCLA Extension several times each year. Wallach is an attorney admitted to the New York Bar and began his career with a short stint in the Queens District Attorney's Office. He quickly shifted to entertainment, working at first in business affairs for RCA Records in New York, and then the legal departments for Capitol Records and Motown Records in Hollywood. Moving into television and film, he was a business affairs executive at Columbia Pictures Television. Additionally, Wallach has been active in increasing the visibility and regard for personal managers as an important part of the Hollywood process, and served two terms as vice president of the Conference of Personal Managers. Wallach frequently lectures at colleges and acting schools in the Los Angeles area emphasizing his belief that actors can make it in Hollywood with talent as well as focus and knowledge of the business, even if they arrive in town without knowing a soul.

He lives in Brentwood, California.

# APPLAUSE FOR
# "HOW TO GET ARRESTED"

"I have young people around me who try to weave through the tangles and get somewhere acting in Los Angeles. As I read this book, I heard the precise emotions that come across my kitchen table and on the phone. Every sigh, cry, laugh and wail. The book is sensible and readable and catches all the nuances of such a tough, complicated business. Michael Wallach commits the grievous error of using common sense. If I were in the business, which I am glad I'm not, this would be my guide and every day. Congratulations on a fine job, one that is a service to these ragamuffins in the outer office waiting to become huge stars."

*Jimmy Breslin*
*Pulitzer Prize winning columnist*

"As a client of Michael Wallach Management, I have relied on his wisdom, expertise, and guidance for years. Now he's put his considerable savvy into a book, and one that's an easy, fun read at that. It's a touchstone for the actor who wants to navigate this very tricky business of ours."

*John Savage, Actor*
*More than 100 feature films and TV productions*
*"The Deerhunter," "The Thin Red Line," James Cameron's "Dark Angel"*

"Michael Wallach's course for UCLA Extension, "This Business of Acting™" has become popular and for good reason – he has a plethora of information and a unique, easy-mannered delivery, both of which are in marvelous evidence in "How to Get Arrested"."

*Jane Kagon, Director*
*Department of Entertainment Studies*
*UCLA Extension*

"This book is utterly charming, informative and unique – a terrific read for anyone who acts or wants to professionally. It is an engaging tale of two actors traveling on two different roads, both pursuing the same dream. The surprises and lessons learned are great not only for the two characters, but for us, the reader. Bravo! A book to enjoy and learn from."

*Joanne Baron,*
*Actress, Acting Coach, Producer*
*Joanne Baron / D. W. Brown Acting Studio*
*Has Coached Halle Berry and Julia Stiles*

"What frequently strikes me about actors is they think because what they do is considered an art form, that their talent alone will propel them to success. The truth is, even the most charismatic actor needs to focus on the business of acting itself to make the climb. They need to know you don't just put on a tight sweater and sit at a lunch counter like Lana Turner and get a movie contract. Lucky for them, Michael Wallach has written this book. It's a genuine blueprint for success, and if many of the actors who audition for me read it, I'm positive their chances to 'make it' will be markedly improved."

*Victoria Burrows, Casting Director*
*More Than 100 Feature Films*
*and TV Productions*
*"The Lord of the Rings" Trilogy*

"Mastering the art of tennis and playing poker are two challenges I'd like to think I've taken on well, but show business is a different sort of competition. Now, 'How to Get Arrested' comes along and gives actors a realistic framework for mastering the art of making it in a game that has an elastic rule book."

*Vince Van Patten, Actor*
*Host, "World Poker Tour"*

"I wish I had this book when I was starting out. It would have saved me a lot of time and heartache. My 17 year old niece wants to be an actress and this book is the gift I'm giving to her."

*Eileen Davidson, Actress*
*Emmy-nominated for "The Young and the Restless"and "Days of Our Lives"*

"I started acting as a kid and even with experience in front of the camera as I got older and had to make career decisions it was still all new. I would ask why there wasn't some book to help. Well, Michael Wallach has finally written that book and even with a lifetime acting, I feel more informed and more self-empowered after reading it."

*Morgan Brittany, Actress*
*"Dallas," "Glitter," "Gypsy"*

"Like no other book – a fun story format reveals nuance and wisdom for the finest possibilities toward success both financial and artistic in Hollywood."

*Steven Nash, Personal Manager*
*President, Talent Managers Association*

"I have been casting film and television for more than 20 years and have seen the many methods actors use in order to be cast. After reading an insightful, motivational, and practical book called 'How to Get Arrested,' I can say unequivocally that this book will be an extremely valuable tool for the actor."

*Jan Glaser, Casting Director*
*More Than 75 Feature Film and TV*
*Productions*

"Some personal managers tell their clients to do the acting and let them take care of business, but I've never subscribed to that theory and neither does Michael Wallach. Instead, with 'How to Get Arrested' he's given actors a primer to understanding how show *business* works. It's a great idea brilliantly executed.

*Tami Lynn, Personal Manager*
*Clients include Christina Applegate*

"I fell in love with Dick and Jane. They are a perfect foil for veteran show biz advisor Michael Wallach's sage advice on how to break into the L.A. scene."

*Carolyn Howard-Johnson, Author*
*"The Frugal Book Promoter: How to Do*
*What Your Publisher Won't"*
*"This Is The Place," "Harkening"*

"My company has been managing actors for more than 30 years in both New York and Los Angeles, and with new clients we always have to try to teach them the business side of their careers. Now we can start by having them read 'How to Get Arrested' -- it's a marvelous, concise book.

*Helene Sokol, Personal Manager*
*Cuzzins Management*

"Michael Wallach's 'How to Get Arrested' is a riveting inside look at the difficult journey of making it as an actor."

*Marv Albert, Sportscaster*

"Show Business is neither easy to understand nor easy to navigate. Within the pages of 'How to Get Arrested' Michael Wallach finds a way to present the 'How to Succeed' in the most accessible way I have ever read. This is a charming story, truly motivational, and the perfect gift for the aspiring actor – and we all know aspiring actors.

*Alan L. Gansberg, Writer-Producer*
*Four-time Emmy nominee*
*Former TV Editor, The Hollywood Reporter*

"What I enjoyed most about 'How to Get Arrested' was the format was so different. It wasn't like the typical how-to-become-an-actor books you normally see. It stands alone. Michael Wallach was able to grab my attention emotionally through the characters of Dick and Jane, who, of course, translate into my own life. His storytelling actually re-energized me."

*Genevieve Lee, Aspiring Actress*
*Student of "This Business of Acting™"*

"I've read the book and I love it.  It is written simply without making anyone wrong, just ignorant.  Most successful actors work at their careers just as Michael Wallach has shown.  The book has the encouragement of a fable like 'The Little Prince' that teaches lessons beautifully.  I am so excited about this book.  It is truly wonderful."

*Judy Kerr, Author*
*"Acting is Everything:  An Actor's*
*Guidebook for a Successful Career in*
*Los Angeles" (10th Edition)*

Printed in the United States
35802LVS00004B/4-54

9 781420 879025